Collaborating for Change

EDITED BY PEGGY HOLMAN AND TOM DEVANE

Real Time Strategic Change

ROBERT W. JACOBS
AND FRANK McKEOWN

Berrett-Koehler Communications, Inc.
8 California Street, Suite 610
San Francisco, CA 94111-4825

ORDERING INFORMATION

Please send orders to Berrett-Koehler Communications, P.O. Box 565, Williston, VT 05495. Or place your order by calling 800-929-2929, faxing 802-864-7626, or visiting www.bkconnection.com.
Special discounts are available on quantity purchases. For details, call 800-929-2929. See the back of this booklet for more information and an order form.

 Printed in the United States of America
on acid-free and recycled paper.

CONTENTS

INTRODUCTION

Voices That Count:
Realizing the Potential of Change

. . . .

Peggy Holman and Tom Devane

As seen through the lens of history, change is inevitable. Just look at any history book. Everything from fashions to attitudes has changed dramatically through the years. Change reflects underlying shifts in values and expectations of the times. Gutenberg's invention of the movable type–printing press in the fifteenth century, for example, bolstered the developing humanism of the Renaissance. The new technology complemented the emerging emphasis on individual expression that brought new developments in music, art, and literature. Economic and political shifts paralleled the changing tastes in the arts, creating a prosperous and innovative age—a stark contrast to the preceding Middle Ages.

On the surface, technology enables greater freedom and prosperity. Yet this century has overwhelmed us with new technologies: automobiles, airplanes, radios, televisions, telephones, computers, the Internet. What distinguishes change today is the turbulence created by the breathtaking pace required to assimilate its effects.

In terms of social change, one trend is clear: people are demanding a greater voice in running their own lives. Demonstrated by the American Revolution and affirmed more recently in the fall of the Berlin Wall, the riots in Tiananmen Square, the social unrest in Indonesia, and the redistribution of power in South Africa, this dramatic shift in values and expectations creates enormous potential for positive change today.

. . . .

So, why does change have such a bad reputation?

One reason is that change introduces uncertainty. While change holds the possibility of good things happening, 80 percent of us see only its negative aspects.[1] And even when people acknowledge their current situation is far from perfect, given the choice between the devil they know or the devil they don't, most opt for the former. The remedy we are learning is to involve people in creating a picture of a better future. Most of us are drawn toward the excitement and possibility of change and move past our fear of the unknown.

Another reason we are wary of change is that it can create winners and losers. Clearly the British were not happy campers at the end of the American Revolution. In corporations, similar battle lines are often drawn between those with something to lose and those with something to gain. The real challenge is to view the change *systemically* and ask what's best for both parties in the post-change environment.

Finally, many people have real data that change is bad for them. These change survivors know that "flavor of the month" change initiatives generally fall disappointingly short. In our organizations and communities, many people have experienced the results of botched attempts at transformational change. Like the cat that jumps on a hot stove only once, it's simple human nature to avoid situations that cause pain. And let's face it, enough change efforts have failed to create plenty of cynicism over the past ten years. For these people, something had better "smell" completely different if they're going to allow themselves to care.

Ironically, as demands for greater involvement in our organizations increased, leaders of many well-publicized, large-scale change efforts moved the other way and totally ignored people. They chose instead to focus on more visible and seemingly easier-to-manage components such as information technology, strategic architectures, and business processes. Indeed, "Downsize" was a ubiquitous battle cry of the nineties. According to a 1996 *New York Times* poll, "Nearly three-quarters of all households have had a close encounter with layoffs since 1980. In one-third of all households, a family member has lost a job, and nearly 40 percent more know a relative, friend, or neighbor who was laid off."[2] The individual impact has been apparent in the increased stress, longer working hours, and reduced sense of job security chronicled in virtually every recent book and article on change.

To paraphrase Winston Churchill, "Never before in the field of human endeavors was so much screwed up by so few for so many." By ignoring the need to involve people in something that affects them, many of today's popular change methods have left a bad taste in the mouths of "change targets" (as one popular methodology calls those affected) for *any* type of change. They have also often left behind less effective organizations with fewer people and lower morale. Consequently, even well-intentioned, well-designed change efforts have a hard time getting off the ground.

If an organization or community's leaders *do* recognize that emerging values and rapidly shifting environmental demands call for directly engaging people in change, they often face another challenge. When the fear of uncertainty, the potential for winners and losers, and the history of failures define change, how can they systematically involve people and have some confidence that it will work? That is where this booklet comes in.

A Way Through

This booklet offers an approach that works because it acknowledges the prevailing attitudes toward change. It offers a fresh view based on the possibility of a more desirable future, experience with the whole system, and activities that signal "something different is happening this time." That difference systematically taps the potential of human beings to make themselves, their organizations, and their communities more adaptive and more effective. This approach is based on solid, proven principles for unleashing people's creativity, knowledge, and spirit toward a common purpose.

How can this be? It does so by filling two huge voids that most large-scale change efforts miss. The first improvement is *intelligently involving people* in changing their workplaces and communities. We have learned that creating a collective sense of purpose, sharing information traditionally known only to a few, valuing what people have to contribute, and inviting them to participate in meaningful ways positively affects outcomes. In other words, informed, engaged people can produce dramatic results.

The second improvement is a *systemic* approach to change. By asking "Who's affected? Who has a stake in this?" we begin to recognize that no change happens in isolation. Making the interdependencies explicit enables shifts based on a common view of the whole. We can each play our part while understanding our contribution to the system. We begin to understand that in a change effort the "one-party-wins-and-one-party-loses" perception need not necessarily be the case. When viewed from a systemic perspective, the lines between "winners" and "losers" become meaningless as everyone participates in cocreating the future for the betterment of all. The advantages are enormous: coordinated actions and closer relationships lead to simpler, more effective solutions.

The growing numbers of success stories are beginning to attract attention. Hundreds of examples around the world of dramatic and sustained increases in organization and community performance now exist.[3] With such great potential, why isn't everyone operating this way? The catch with high-involvement, systemic change is that more people have their say. Until traditional managers are ready to say yes to that, no matter how stunning the achievements of others, these approaches will remain out of reach for most and a competitive advantage for a few.

Our Purpose

This booklet describes an approach that has helped others achieve dramatic, sustainable results in their organization or communities. Our purpose is to provide basic information that you can use to decide whether this approach is right for you. We give you an overview including an illustrative story, answers to frequently asked questions and tips for getting started. We've also given you discussion questions for "thinking aloud" with others and a variety of references to learn more.

There is ample evidence that when high involvement and a system-wide approach are used, the potential for unimagined results is within reach. As Goethe so eloquently reminds us, "Whatever you can do or dream you can, begin it. Boldness has genius, power, and magic in it."

What are you waiting for?

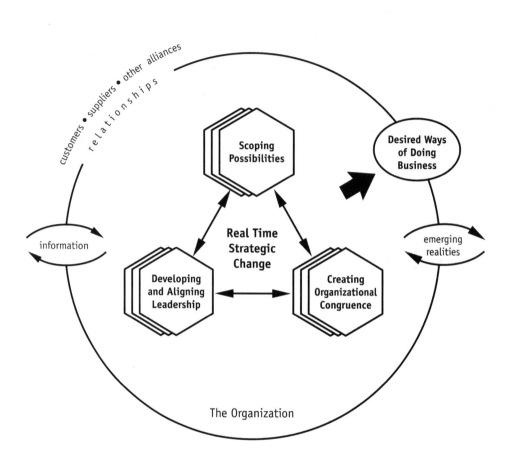

customers • suppliers • other alliances

relationships

Scoping
Possibilities

Desired Ways
of Doing
Business

Real Time
Strategic
Change

information

Developing
and Aligning
Leadership

Creating
Organizational
Congruence

emerging
realities

The Organization

RealTime Strategic Change

*I know of no safe depository of the ultimate powers of the society
but the people themselves, and if we think them not enlightened
enough to exercise their control with a wholesome discretion,
the remedy is not to take it from them, but to inform their discretion.*

—THOMAS JEFFERSON, SEPTEMBER 28, 1820

A $750 million regional business unit of a multinational oil and gas
company needed a rapid turnaround or risked being sold off. In
response, a Real Time Strategic Change[SM] (RTSC[SM])[1] effort was
launched, including more than 20 working sessions of 20 to 1,000 people. The sessions focused on strategy development, organization
design, core process redesign, launch of a new business, and commitment to a unified team.

In August 1995, 1,000 people (85 percent of the organization) met
for three days. The group developed a strategy to integrate three separate organizations and reached consensus on action items needed for
improving performance. These action items were designed to break a
vicious cycle that had trapped the organization for the past five years
(see Figure 1).

Ten months later the business unit was reorganized around core
processes. Return on fixed assets increased 15 percent (9 percent
adjusted for price), cycle time reductions saved $30 million; capital
spending overage dropped from $70 million to zero, a new business is
generating $12 million and has led to a 30 percent reduction in a major

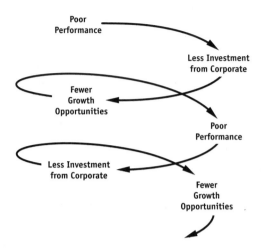

Figure 1. Vicious Cycle

recurring expenditure, and five deep-water leases were secured—a first for the business. A culture of mistrust and parochialism was transformed to one of collaboration. The business unit was not sold off.

Chris Christensen, the business unit general manager, reflected:

> We had three different business units in approximately the same location, but we weren't functioning as a single entity, and more important, we weren't competitive in the marketplace.
>
> Thirty people from all levels and functions, including elected union officials, came to a Real Time Strategic Change training course. On the second evening we all got together and identified over 30 different potential applications for RTSC. Everyone decided we had to use this approach because it was how we wanted to work together in the future . . . and we could make that happen fast.
>
> Our leadership team joined forces with a design team to determine the business strategy and how to design this as an overall effort. When we finally brought 1,000 people together, I

watched one huge leadership team debate the issues and find answers on its own. I was proud of the issues they picked, even deciding how people needed to work with each other in the new organization. That was a big turning point.

Then a group of 80, some representing a microcosm of the organization and others with project planning expertise, came together and translated recommendations from the meeting of 1,000 into six core work processes. Other teams charged with developing the process designs reached into the organization to include people. They went to offshore platforms for feedback instead of making folks who wanted to participate come to them. Little things like this sent a strong message about how business would be done from now on.

By April 1996, the new organization was up and running. New process leaders had been chosen by a microcosm of the organization. Process-based teams had come together and reviewed, developed, and agreed on their individual parts of the new structure and on their key relationships.

. . . . .

Bill Buchanan, hired as Sedgwick County manager in January 1991, began, "The county was full of fiefdoms, suspicion, and bureaucratic personnel systems. People were eager to change, but we didn't have a common direction or purpose."

Jerry Harrison, assistant county manager, continued, "We started using RTSC to find our direction and begin focusing on improving service to the community. For the first time we included stakeholders in our planning process: citizens, neighboring municipalities, and local businesses. Then we started including citizens in community discussions about everything from trash disposal to new voting machines."

"From an employee perspective," said internal consultant Kristi Zukovich, "this work took us to a more professional level. We think every day about the results we need to achieve and the actions that will get us there. We now focus on how can we find new ways to compete and add value to the community."

Harrison said, "The county provides funding to local agencies serving physically and mentally challenged people. Several agencies wanted our money and they all had waiting lists . . . so our citizens' needs were not being met. We met with agency providers, clients, and their family members. As a result, we've put the purchasing power into the clients' hands so they can buy services from the providers they want. With this spending power, clients are getting better services and we're getting a better return on our investment. Examples like this run throughout the county—our focus on service delivery has intensified significantly."

"We've also created what is now a nationwide model for homeless services in communities," concluded Buchanan. "The state has contracted with us to train others in involving stakeholders in areas like juvenile crime. We even have other states calling us for help. For us, we're just doing business the only way we know how anymore."

What Is Real Time Strategic Change?

Real Time Strategic Change is a principle-based approach that makes it possible to achieve rapid, sustainable, organization-wide change. *Rapid* means bringing your preferred future into the present—thinking and acting as if the future were now. *Sustainable* means that an organization can adapt and continue to be successful as new realities emerge.

RTSC is an approach that engages organizations and their members as living systems, focusing on spirit and community as well as on strategies, structures, and processes. However, RTSC is not just an approach to organization-wide change. It is also a way of doing business, a way of thinking and acting on a daily basis. Seeing change in this way, as a normal part of doing business, is an example of the paradoxical thinking that permeates the RTSC approach.

Principles form RTSC's foundation—the solid and fixed basis of the approach. The six RTSC principles (see Figure 2) support lasting change because they provide guidance in any situation—for change work and for daily work as well.

Having *only* six principles provides focus and clarity, guiding choices during and beyond change efforts. Being principle-based allows great flexibility in application so that organizations can shape unique pathways to their future. The principles allow RTSC to operate as an "open platform," creating possibilities for leverage and synergy with any other approaches to organizational change and development that are congruent with them.

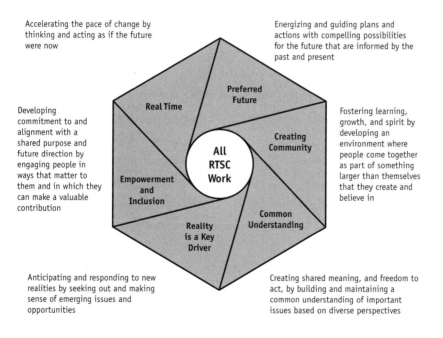

Figure 2. Real Time Strategic Change Principles

Martin Raff led a systemwide RTSC effort as a regional director in the United Kingdom's Employment Service. He highlights the principles' broad application, saying, "Leaders at all organizational levels use the RTSC principles in their daily work of leading, planning, problem solving, and dealing with employees, customers, shareholders, and the community."

When to Consider Using RTSC

In considering whether to use RTSC, it does not matter what kind of change you are making, how complex or unclear the issues or courses of action are, or even what the size of the organization is. What does matter is that the issues are fundamental to the organization, rapid change is preferred, leadership is open to new ideas about the organization's future and how to achieve it, and the leaders believe in sharing power with people at all levels of the organization. RTSC is at its best when there is a sense of urgency and lasting change is the goal.

Typical applications include the following:

Situation	RTSC Application
Issues are complex, chronic, or ill-defined; they span separate parts of the organization; workable solutions seem unattainable	Engaging key stakeholders in clarifying issues, defining purpose and scope, and deciding how to address them
The organization is pulling in different directions; there are mixed messages about who we are, where we are headed	Developing and implementing strategy and achieving rapid results
Current skills and knowledge are insufficient; many people need new competencies	Accelerating the pace of learning through large-group training and development focused on daily work
New technologies and systems, such as enterprise-wide management, are being introduced	Working with entire organization in design and implementation
Organizational mergers, acquisitions, or alliances are occurring; people may feel resentment, fear, or marginalization	Building on strategic and cultural strengths of both organizations to establish a new identity and create productive relationships

Situation	RTSC Application
Business process redesign is being implemented—with new processes, systems, roles, and perhaps downsizing	Involving people in understanding strategy, redefining the organization, and redesigning their core work
Labor and management are seeking breakthroughs in chronic, adversarial, unproductive relationships	Fostering sustainable partnerships based on discovering shared interests and working collaboratively

Table 1. Typical Applications

Ian Peters, manager of organization development and learning at a commercial aircraft assembly manufacturer, said, "We've used RTSC successfully to support work with a merger, to stimulate a lot of innovative thinking about responding to our customers' needs, and to expand what we used to call training to broader organizational change."

How RTSC Works

Organizations navigate their way through three phases in RTSC efforts: Scoping Possibilities, Developing and Aligning Leadership, and Creating Organizational Congruence. Figure 3 shows how RTSC is embedded in an organization's daily work and how cycles of these three phases generate more and more desired ways of doing business.

These ways of doing business are concrete expressions of an organization's preferred future, including how people work with and relate to each other as well as with customers, suppliers, owners, and other key partners. In RTSC, organizations are seen as open systems connected with the world around them through a continual information flow, key stakeholder relationships, and an acute awareness of emerging realities.

Scoping Possibilities is about crafting a clear, considered plan for a change effort. It energizes people with many possibilities for moving their change effort forward. This expansive mode complements the focus people require to create a unique pathway that fits their organization's culture, needs, and constraints. For most organizations, creating

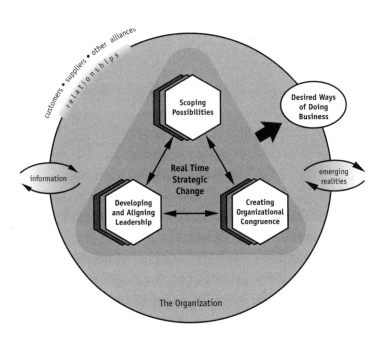

Figure 3. How RTSC Works—
Achieving Sustainable Organizational Performance

their own road map for change is an important part of the experience of doing business in a new way and symbolizes the future.

Developing and Aligning Leadership is about building leadership competencies and commitment required for a successful change effort and for congruent leadership in the future. These capabilities can be grown in a number of possible ways and settings: large-scale events, smaller retreats, action learning initiatives, individual reflection and coaching sessions, training sessions, and daily work with other leaders and the larger organization. These efforts focus on developing a pre-ferred and consistent leadership style, strategy alignment, and a range of skills including leading and supporting implementation of desired ways of doing business.

In this phase, leaders develop and align around the case for change and the organization's future direction. They also decide how and when to engage other members in this work. For example, leaders sometimes choose to develop strategy themselves and engage others later in understanding and translating it to daily work. In other cases, they choose to involve people immediately and develop strategy together from a "clean sheet." More broadly, deciding how and when to share power and authority is an important, conscious, ongoing process that begins in this phase.

Creating Organizational Congruence is about engaging the entire organization in developing a solid fit among the following:

- external realities
- the preferred future
- strategy and plans
- systems, structures, and processes
- daily work

This phase begins with communicating to the organization the purpose, scope, scale, and plan for the change effort. Support initiatives for change, focusing on the items above, typically include RTSC events as well as teams, task forces, processes, and methods suited to the particular initiative. Over time, what is learned in this phase translates into better ways of thinking and acting on a daily basis.

RTSC events, roll-up-your-sleeves working sessions, are a cornerstone of this phase of work. RTSC technologies work for small groups as well as for groups of 1,000 or more. Whether for reaching consensus on strategic direction or developing and applying new competencies to real issues, these events realize the power and possibilities of the collective, way beyond what is possible with more traditional methods.

What You Can Expect to Achieve Using RTSC

Dramatic quantitative and qualitative gains are often a direct result of RTSC efforts, as the stories that open the chapter show. Given RTSC's flexibility and variety of potential applications, a large range of outcomes is possible. Tim Jones, managing director of Retail Bank Services for National Westminster Bank in England, captured the spirit of his organization's RTSC work by saying, "We were seeking a way to achieve real dialogue within our business—these [RTSC] ideas created a real breakthrough in engaging our people in success."

Clear strategic alignment across the organization makes it possible to move forward on many fronts at once. Synergies emerge unpredictably among previously unrelated initiatives and commonly lead to discovering unknown problems. Janice Saunders, an area director in the United Kingdom's Employment Service, attributes an £18 million annual savings to an RTSC effort in which the scope of a previously ignored issue became clear. This led to relatively straightforward process and system changes, resulting in these significant cost savings.

RTSC increases collaboration and trust in an organization. Ian Paterson of Strategy Management Consultants in South Africa said, "We have managers in many organizations with an individualistic, profit-oriented approach. In contrast, much of the workforce has a traditional African approach based on 'Ubuntu,' or collective humanism. RTSC combines both approaches, engaging the collective spirit while also recognizing individual needs and business aspirations."

RTSC is often the catalyst for personal change. Jerry Harrison of Sedgwick County said, "The process of involving others was a pretty dramatic change for me. I used to make more decisions myself and spent a lot of time selling my ideas to others. Now I don't have to convince anybody that I've made a good decision. When 'we' make the decisions, they're usually good ones."

The ultimate reward from RTSC work is sustainable performance, uniquely defined and measured by each organization using both hard numbers and qualitative organizational health and well-being assessments. It shows up in organizations that are valued as places to learn, grow, belong, and contribute, with well-understood values and norms. It shows up in the awareness and assessment of changing marketplace moods and shifts and of how and when to respond to these shifts.

Getting Started with RTSC

RTSC efforts sometimes begin with a goal of fundamental and wide-spread change. More commonly, organizations see a need for involving large numbers of their members in addressing specific issues and opportunities. In each case, a good way to start is for an organization to explore

- its issues and opportunities and their underlying assumptions,
- potential key players and their possible roles,
- existing initiatives and any linkages to this proposed effort,
- images of what a good result would be from an effort,
- options about the scope and scale of the undertaking (limits and boundaries),
- ideas for moving forward.

This initial scoping is best done by a representative group of the organization that may include formal and informal leaders, internal and external consultants, organization members, and even external stakeholders. This should be a practical mix of people with the information, interest, and innovative thinking needed to develop a solid appreciation of the organization's situation.

Challenging conventional thinking, current practices, assumptions, and norms with "What if . . . ?" scenarios during this early stage helps establish a preferred future orientation. It also helps avoid the trap of just taking today's issues and trying to solve them with a business-as-usual approach. Mike Weiss, a key player in a change effort at Brooklyn Technical High School involving curriculum redesign, faculty development, and facilities management, said, "Very early on, we began questioning things we'd always taken for granted. In most schools, the principal announces changes. We're taking a different tack by working side-by-side with the faculty in redesigning Tech. If we want to be partnering with teachers and other key players, why not start doing it now?"

We know from experience that people's commitment to and involvement in RTSC efforts have a habit of snowballing, radically accelerating the pace and breadth of implementation. Therefore, it's essential to be several steps ahead of the system, being ready to help people develop supportive leadership, explore scenarios for how the effort might evolve, and consider well-thought-through resource planning. As change efforts progress, much occurs as planned and predicted, be it data gathering by a task force, process redesign, or a large event. Other aspects of the work are emergent and unpredictable, such as how and when early images of a preferred future begin influencing how scoping work proceeds or new business practices surface.

Roles and Structures in an RTSC Effort

Roles and structures are uniquely designed to meet the needs and constraints of each organization's RTSC effort. Some can be planned, while others emerge as the work unfolds.

For example, at a telecommunications company, an event-design team decided that all 10,000 employees needed to understand vital information within a two-week window. While the company's communications staff doubted the feasibility of this, it worked with the design team and organized dozens of large, interactive meetings. People attending the meetings were impressed with the quality of their experience. They were even more impressed that the design team members had taken it upon themselves to make inroads into the chronic problem of people's "not really knowing what's going on."

Some of an RTSC effort's more common roles and structures are discussed below:

Initial Scoping Group and Change Effort Design Team: An initial scoping group does the early thinking about whether and how to move forward. Once there is agreement between client and consultants to proceed, a change effort design team is usually formed. It's best if both structures are a representative microcosm of the organization, but they should not necessarily have the same membership. A change effort design team determines the critical path, key initiatives, and plans for the overall effort, often collaborating widely in this work. Over time, the change effort plan is revised, sometimes radically, based on data-gathering initiatives, regular reflection/learning sessions, and unscheduled, real-time responses to emerging issues and opportunities.

Leaders and Leadership Teams: Formal and often informal leaders partner with other key stakeholders to draft strategy, create and support emerging ways of doing business, and communicate the case for change to people throughout the organization. They discover and develop a leadership style that is congruent with the organization's preferred future. They also engage with the larger organization in ongoing dialogues about important issues such as authority, roles, and decision making; the organization's values and norms and how these translate into daily work; development, interpretation, and implementation of strategy; preferred futures in action; and communication and information flows.

Event and Initiative Design Teams: Organized as microcosms of the larger organization, these teams plan and manage the content and processes for RTSC events and initiatives, such as event agendas, benchmarking surveys, organizational-design efforts, and communications support.

Logistics Teams: Members are charged with everything from seamlessly managing audio quality for events to producing meeting materials, documenting event output, or supporting development of internal communications, such as an intranet.

Organization Members: In addition to potentially joining any of the above teams, organization members have at least two other roles in RTSC efforts: (1) working on systemwide issues and opportunities in RTSC events, and (2) implementing desired ways of doing business in their daily work. They may also be working on support initiatives of different types in short-term or more enduring teams.

Consultants: Internal consultants and external consultants specializing in change, strategy, redesign, information technology, and other specialties need to partner closely in RTSC work. RTSC consultant competencies include the ability to

- work from the RTSC principles and translate them into action;
- consult on and implement RTSC processes and practices, such as large-scale events;
- identify and manage polarities[2] and build client capability to do the same;
- help clients discover opportunities to realize their future faster;
- use a keen understanding of complex systems to identify leverage points for change;
- appreciate transformation and its impact on individuals, teams, and the larger organization;
- support systemwide changes taking place simultaneously.

RTSC's Impact on Power and Authority

Power and authority issues impact nearly every facet of organizational change. RTSC efforts bring to light existing assumptions about power and authority, establish new ones as needed, and redefine roles and relationships to share power in highly functional and effective ways.

There is no good way to "solve" the question Should leaders be directive or participative? This issue is a typical and important example of a polarity that needs to be continually managed (because it can't be solved). RTSC's impact on power and authority issues leads to cultures that are both participative *and* directive—another example of paradoxical thinking.

There are upsides and downsides to all polarities (see Figure 4). The paradoxical nature of polarities means that overfocusing on one pole, say, becoming more participative, will eventually result in experiencing the downside of that same pole. Effective management in this case means achieving more of the positive dimensions of direction *and*

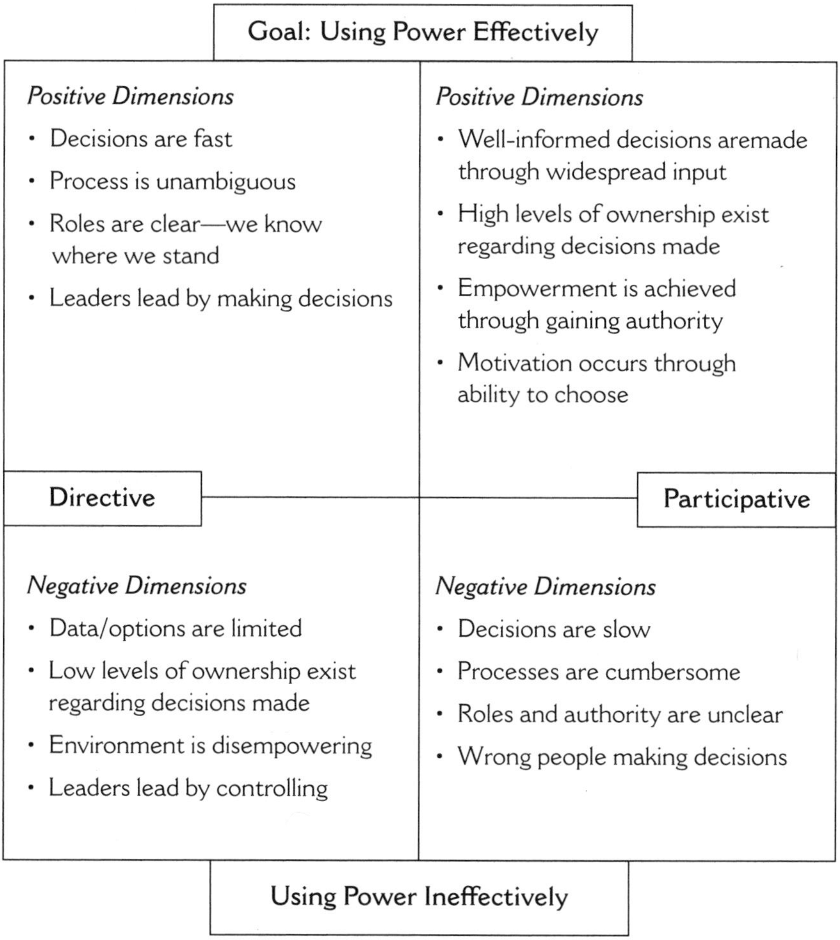

Goal: Using Power Effectively

Positive Dimensions

- Decisions are fast
- Process is unambiguous
- Roles are clear—we know where we stand
- Leaders lead by making decisions

Positive Dimensions

- Well-informed decisions aremade through widespread input
- High levels of ownership exist regarding decisions made
- Empowerment is achieved through gaining authority
- Motivation occurs through ability to choose

Directive | Participative

Negative Dimensions

- Data/options are limited
- Low levels of ownership exist regarding decisions made
- Environment is disempowering
- Leaders lead by controlling

Negative Dimensions

- Decisions are slow
- Processes are cumbersome
- Roles and authority are unclear
- Wrong people making decisions

Using Power Ineffectively

Figure 4. Polarity Map™

participation while minimizing their negative aspects. RTSC supports clients in understanding the nature of polarities and in developing effective strategies for their management.

Conditions for Success

The following factors are critical to achieving sustainable success in an RTSC effort:

1. Thinking and acting with the whole change effort in mind leads to
   - individual decisions and actions congruent with the overall effort;
   - a clear purpose, desired results, and a plan responsive to emerging realities that provide the road map for moving forward; and
   - an awareness that although phenomenal results are achievable solely from RTSC events, they alone are unlikely to lead to lasting change.

2. Formal and informal leaders need to
   - demonstrate visible, tangible commitment to the effort;
   - dedicate time, energy, and significant organizational resources; and
   - do their daily work in ways that are congruent with the organization's preferred future.

3. Profound levels of inclusion and empowerment of people—designing and implementing their change efforts, developing support initiatives, creating strategies, and deciding courses of action—are hallmarks of the RTSC approach. Mere exposure and participation by many or substantial immersion by a few rarely results in broad ownership or good strategic decisions.

4. Processes, systems, and structures need to reflect and reinforce actions that move the organization toward its preferred future.

Not addressing these fundamental aspects of organizational life is making a choice for cosmetic change.

5. RTSC work requires solid partnering among the client organization, RTSC practitioners, and expert consultants who may be involved. This partnering needs to continually evolve based on shared values, clear expectations, and regular reflection. Organizational members lead their own change efforts, influencing the way RTSC practitioners work as the practitioners influence the organization.

Historical Context of RTSC

Real Time Strategic Change has evolved from a diverse mix of disciplines that we have organized into five categories: time, learning, change, systems, and performance (see Figure 5).

The main history of RTSC development follows.

Kurt Lewin's group dynamics work in the 1940s and 1950s and Dick Beckhard, Ron Lippitt, and Eva Schindler-Rainman's contributions with large groups in the 1960s and 1970s form the early roots of the RTSC approach. Russ Ackoff, Peter Checkland, and Ian Mitroff's Systems Thinking concepts are a core construct of RTSC. Malcolm Knowles, K. Patricia Cross, and David Kolb's adult-learning theories provide frameworks that shape RTSC's practice.

The work of Kathie Dannemiller, Al Davenport, Bruce Gibb, and Chuck Tyson with internal consultants Nancy Badore and Cynthia Holm that supported Tom Page's culture-change effort at Ford in the early 1980s marked another stage of development. Our work and that of our colleagues at Dannemiller Tyson Associates through the early 1990s led to broader applications of this large-scale approach, described in *Real Time Strategic Change: How to Involve an Entire Organization in Fast and Far-Reaching Change*, by Robert W. Jacobs (Berrett-Koehler, 1994).

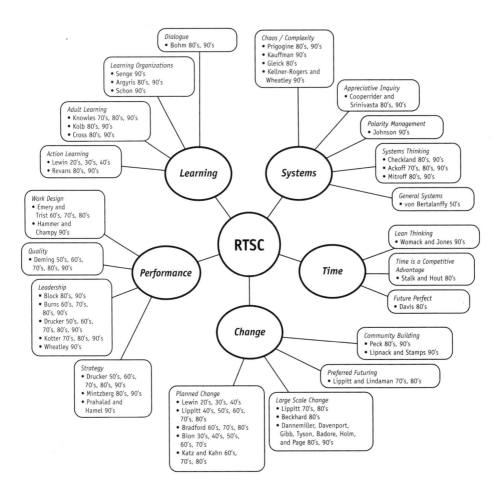

Figure 5. Schools of Thought Influencing RTSC's Development

Since then, RTSC concepts and practice have evolved substantially. One of the major advances has been a shift from an event-centered technology to a change-effort-focused approach, of which events are a part. The most significant advance has been redefining the basis of the RTSC approach from processes to principles, leading to greater flexibility in application and greater sustainability of outcomes. These innovations, reflecting a more profound and broader application of systems thinking, are a direct response to clients' needs.

Stan Davis's contribution of "managing in the 'future perfect' tense" and our translation of James Womack and Daniel Jones's "lean thinking" concepts have profoundly shaped the RTSC approach. These cycle-time-reduction ideas have focused us on supporting clients in embedding desired ways of doing business and in making this happen sooner.

Ilya Prigogine, Stuart Kauffman, Meg Wheatley, and Myron Kellner-Rogers have influenced our thinking on chaos, complexity, and self-organizing systems. Their ideas have shaped and affirmed the emergent nature of RTSC work, in particular its relationship to the areas of field theory and complex adaptive systems.

Barry Johnson's work on Polarity Management™ supports sustainability in two ways: organizations learn how to effectively manage polarities and how to avoid never-ending cycles of trying to solve unsolvable problems. He describes the RTSC principles as "key polarities that need to be managed well in order to achieve sustainable change."

RTSC and Sustainability

Sustainability, an organization's capability to adapt and continue to be successful as new realities emerge, is not achievable without special focus and investment made at the very outset of change. It must be a way of thinking that influences the scope, architecture, and implementation of change efforts, specific initiatives, and even daily work.

Without up-front attention to making the results of change last, follow-up plans to maintain momentum not only do not achieve desired results but also, paradoxically, can detract from them. Follow-up plans reinforce the paradigm that change work is not real work. Indeed, the perceived need for developing follow-up plans to initiatives such as large-scale events can signal that the organization is designed not to support desired change. In such circumstances, people tend to feel that working on change is not their job.

Sustainability is deeply embedded in all aspects of RTSC work. It is built into how scoping work is approached, change-effort plans are developed, and systemwide changes are made. It is about tools and approaches that help translate desired ways of doing business right into daily work, making them part of the culture.

Julie Beedon of VISTA Consulting (Europe), important contributors to RTSC's evolution, said, "Through an RTSC approach, organizations succeed because they learn to adapt in real time to environmental changes. You see it happening in different parts of the organization as well as at a systemwide level. Over time, this type of adaptiveness becomes a natural mode of operating."

Sustainability also depends on how well an organization manages those issues that have no right answers: Team or individual? Directive or participative? Present or future? Owners or members? By effectively managing these polarities, organizations can avoid the typical swings between poles that undermine sustainable progress.

Most important, sustainability is about organizations and their members developing competencies needed to identify and implement future changes while they navigate their way through current changes.

Bill Buchanan of Sedgwick County said, "Change in the county has been about . . . continual learning, innovation, and daily partnering with our stakeholders. Early on, as we moved toward these things they made sense to us in our heads and at a gut level. Now they're as much a part of who we are as what we do—that's what lasting change is about."

Practical Guide to Real Time Strategic Change

Here is a chance for you to get a "hands-on" experience of applying RTSC to issues and opportunities in your organization or community. Better understanding of the principles and phases of work can help ensure your success.

Using the RTSC Principles[3]

The principles form the foundation of all RTSC work. They can be used in four main ways:

- To guide the design of a process or initiative from scratch or to address a particular issue, for example, "How could we design this process or initiative so that it is in line with the principles?"
- To inform decisions at all levels in a change effort, for example, "How well does this decision align with the principles?"
- To "audit" the desired outcomes in order to determine if the RTSC approach is a good fit, for example, "How well do the RTSC principles match the outcomes/future/vision we desire?"
- To guide better ways of doing business in daily work situations, for example, "If we were acting on the principles, how might we do this work differently?"

Six-Step Process to Apply the Principles

Step 1: Bring together a group of interested and affected stakeholders.

Step 2: Put the situation, decision, or dilemma in the center of the principles hexagon (see Figure 2).

Step 3: Build a common picture of how the principles, individually and collectively, relate to the situation.

- Which principles are most congruent (best fit) with the current situation? How?
- Which ones appear to be least congruent?

Step 4: Reflecting on this, find ways to more fully apply the principles.

- How can those least connected to the situation be leveraged?
- How can those that fit best be built upon?

Step 5: Identify intended *and* possible unintended consequences of ideas the group agrees on.

Step 6: Agree on next steps that could include

- communicating findings and ideas to key stakeholders,
- making action plans, and
- documenting learnings for others.

Implementing the RTSC Phases

Scoping Possibilities

This is an ongoing process of gaining broad appreciation among key stakeholders of needs, interests, possibilities, and issues. The deliverable is a draft plan, or "roadmap," for the change effort.

Six-Step Scoping Process[4]

Step 1: Develop a "key stakeholder map" with the overall issue in the center:

- Key stakeholders are identified by answering: "Who can significantly impact or be impacted by this issue?" Also note on your map "What is their stake in this issue?"
- Share the thinking behind the positioning of stakeholders relative to each other and to the issue.
- This data will help identify representation for the design team.

Step 2: The design team should map the relationships between the overall issue and other initiatives proposed or under way in the organization. This identifies linkages needed among different initiatives and avoids redundancy and missed opportunities.

Step 3: Build a solid assessment of the current situation—what's working and not working.

Step 4: Focus on results to be achieved from your effort—outcomes and purpose.[3]

- What realistic and achievable outcomes can also provide a "stretch" for people? What will serve as useful stepping-stones between current reality and your preferred future?
- What overarching purpose captures these outcomes in language that is easily understood?

Step 5: Brainstorm activities, initiatives and events that could enable you to achieve your purpose, fit your organization's desired culture, and represent better ways of doing business.

Step 6: Critically select and sequence these elements into a roadmap that links to other initiatives identified in Step 2.

- What resources will be needed and when?
- How can the plan engage more and more people in the organization—and outside it—in creating their preferred future?
- What are the typical "dropped balls" and "loose ends" in major initiatives in the organization? What needs to happen to foster sustainability?

Developing and Aligning Leadership

Building leadership competencies and commitment is required for a successful change effort and for congruent leadership in the future. Although outlined sequentially, these steps are highly interdependent and their order will vary.

Four-Step Leadership Process

Step 1: Identify the leaders needed for this effort.

- Expanding beyond formal leaders, who in the organization can offer critical support, assistance and direction?

- From a "preferred future" perspective, who would be providing leadership for this effort? How would they be providing leadership? How can you begin partnering with these people now?

Step 2: What do leaders need to align around—for example, preferred future, strategy, leadership style, roles, boundary conditions, resources needed for the effort?

Step 3: What development needs do leaders identify?

Step 4: What methods will best support the work of this phase—retreats, action learning, mentoring and coaching, training?

Creating Organizational Congruence

Engage the entire organization in aligning around its external realities, preferred future, strategy and plans, systems, structures, processes, and daily work. RTSC events play a major part in this phase.

The Three Key Steps

Step 1: The design team must appreciate the larger context (that is, the change effort purpose and plan) within which the event exists. What do we know about boundary conditions, the case for change, preferred future, stakeholders' needs, work schedules, customer demands, resource limitations, and other relevant factors?

Step 2: Develop the event design by using the questions that follow. Plan logistics support well and early.

- What is the "current state" of the organization?
- What assumptions, beliefs, and stories shape how people think and act?
- What outcomes and purpose would capture participants' energy and commitment?
- Who should be attending, and how should they work together?

- What issues, opportunities, and agreements should the group focus on?
- What high-impact work can they do together that they could never do apart?
- What would people be capable of accomplishing at different stages in the event?
- What information and experiences would they need to make good decisions?
- What commitments need to be made, and by whom, for people to believe that real changes are being made and can be sustained?

Step 3: During the event

- Be prepared to respond to emergent needs and emergent data.
- Invariably, the design will need to be redesigned as data emerges.

Notes

. . . .

Introduction

[1] Oakley, Ed, and Doug Krug. *Enlightened Leadership.* Denver, Colo.: Stone Tree Publishing, 1991, p. 38.

[2] The *New York Times, The Downsizing of America.* New York: Times Books, 1996.

[3] Holman, Peggy, and Tom Devane, eds. *The Change Handbook: Group Methods for Shaping the Future.* San Francisco: Berrett-Koehler Publishers, 1999. This book contains over twenty such stories of stellar results from high-involvement, systemic change.

Real Time Strategic Change

[1] Real Time Strategic Change and RTSC are service marks of *5 oceans, inc.*

[2] Polarities are interdependent opposites that need each other for sustainable success over time, e.g., supporting teamwork *and* fostering individual initiative.

[3] Helpful tools for working with the principles and for developing purpose statements are available at our Web site at www.5oceans.com.

[4] The tools of Appreciative Inquiry are a valuable resource in the Scoping Possibilities phase (see booklet in this series) and generally in the practice of RTSC.

Where to Go for More Information

. . . .

Since our focus has been to give you an *introduction* to Real Time Strategic Change, we want you to know where to go for more information. Here are books, articles, Web sites, and other sources that can help you develop a more in-depth understanding. In addition, we have provided recommendations of works that have influenced us.

Organization

5 oceans, inc.
6027 Tory Lane
Chelsea, MI 48118-9437
(734) 475-4215
(734) 475-1068 (fax)
info@5oceans.com (e-mail)   www.5oceans.com

Real Time Strategic Change References

For an extended reading list, call *5 oceans, inc.* or visit the on-line campus at www.rtscnet.com.

Jacobs, Robert W. *Real Time Strategic Change: How to Involve an Entire Organization in Fast and Far-Reaching Change.* San Francisco: Berrett-Koehler, 1994.

This how-to book describes a step-by-step road map for the planning, preparation, and facilitation of RTSC events.

Real Time Strategic Change Global Learning Community: Internal and external consultants and change leaders come together virtually and face-to-face to support each other in live case studies, reflect on work completed, get specific questions answered, and receive mentoring. The on-line campus is located at www.rtscnet.com.

Influential Sources

Ackoff, Russell. *Creating the Corporate Future: Plan or Be Planned For.* New York: John Wiley & Sons, 1981.

The systems thinking contributions of Russell Ackoff, as well as Peter Checkland and Ian Mitroff, permeate all aspects of the thinking and practice of RTSC.

Dannemiller, Kathleen D., and Robert W. Jacobs. "Changing the Way Organizations Change: A Revolution of Common Sense." In *The Journal of Applied Behavioral Science,* vol. 28, no. 4 (December 1992).

This article describes the history and several case applications of Large Scale Change technology as an approach to large-group interventions.

Davis, Stanley. *Future Perfect.* Reading, Mass.: Addison-Wesley, 1987.

Davis's concepts about time have had a strong influence on the RTSC approach and the Real Time principle's emphasis on "being in the future now."

Drucker, Peter. *Adventures of a Bystander (Trailblazers: Rediscovering the Pioneers of Business).* New York: John Wiley & Sons, 1998.

Drucker's thinking has been a consistent source of insight into the challenges faced by our clients in leading large and complex organizations.

———. *The Practice of Management.* New York: Harper & Row, 1954.

Gleick, James. *Chaos: Making of a New Science.* New York: Penguin, 1988.

The work of pioneers in complexity and chaos theory shape our view of organizations as living systems and how they function, learn, adapt, and transform.

Johnson, Barry. *Polarity Management: Identifying and Managing Unsolvable Problems.* Amherst, Mass.: HRD Press, 1992.

Barry Johnson, Ph.D., has pioneered a powerful approach to effectively address seemingly unsolvable problems. Managing these polarities effectively provides a solid foothold on the path to sustainable change. Information sources include Polarity Management Associates (616) 698-0271 and www.polaritymanagement.com.

Jusela, Gary, et al. "Work Innovations at Ford Motor Company." In *Quality, Productivity and Innovation Strategies for Gaining Competitive Advantage,* edited by Y. K. Shetty and V. M. Buehler. New York: Elsevier Science Publishing, 1987.

The concepts and practices developed at Ford in the early 1980s by Kathie Dannemiller, et al., provide an important foundation of our RTSC event work.

Kauffman, Stuart. *At Home in the Universe: The Search for the Laws of Self-Organization and Complexity.* New York: Oxford University Press, 1995.

Lindaman, E., and R. Lippitt. *Choosing the Future You Prefer: A Goal Setting Guide.* Ann Arbor, Mich.: Human Resource Development Associates of Ann Arbor, Michigan, 1979.

Schindler-Rainman, Eva, and Ron Lippitt. *Building the Collaborative Community: Mobilizing Citizens for Action.* Riverside, Calif.: University of California Extension, 1980.

Wheatley, Margaret J. *Leadership and the New Science: Learning About Organization from an Orderly Universe.* San Francisco: Berrett-Koehler, 1992.

Wheatley, Margaret J., and Myron Kellner-Rogers. *A Simpler Way.* San Francisco: Berrett-Koehler, 1996.

Questions for Thinking Aloud

. . . .

To gain additional value from this booklet, consider discussing it with others. Here are some questions you might find useful as you explore Real Time Strategic Change and its application to your situation.

1. What were your reasons for reading about RTSC in the first place? What situation(s) did you have in mind as possible applications?

2. We've learned that six conditions can help you gauge how and if you whould move forward with RTSC work. Where does your organization fit on the scale for each one?

   a. The issues are fundamental to the organization:

Doesn't even rate one star $1-2-3-4-5$ Nothing could be more essential

   b. Rapid change is preferred:

Turtles move too fast $1-2-3-4-5$ Light speed, please!

   c. Leadership is open to new ideas about the organization's future and how to achieve it:

Maybe the bathroom colors could be changed? $1-2-3-4-5$ The slate is clean

   d. Leaders believe in sharing power with people at all levels of the organization:

My way or the highway! $1-2-3-4-5$ Partnership in all we do

   e. There is a sense of urgency:

Relax, there's plenty of time $1-2-3-4-5$ We need to move or lose!

   f. Lasting change is the goal:

Let's get this over with so we can $1-2-3-4-5$ Commitment and resources
get back to real work   say this is for real

3. Did reading the booklet trigger ideas/thoughts for you about your situation (other ways to think about it, other potential applications)? What were they?

4. There are six RTSC principles: Preferred Future, Creating Community, Common Understanding, Reality Is a Key Driver, Empowerment and Inclusion, and Real Time.

   • Where do you see evidence of individual RTSC principles in the daily work of the organization?[1]

   • Which are least visible, or are even at cross-purposes with the culture and how business gets done?

   • How well do the principles fit (individually and collectively) with the desired future for the organization?

5. What unique value could RTSC create for you? If you were to use this approach, what hopes do you have for what you could achieve?

6. What limitations do you see for RTSC's application to your situation? If you were to use this approach, what concerns would you have for the future?

7. What else do you need to do (next steps) to continue your exploration and learning? Who else might you need to engage in this discussion?

Note

[1] For a more in-depth exploration, a description of "What the Principles Mean Day-to-Day" is on our Web site at www.5oceans.com.

The Authors

. . . .

Robert W. Jacobs (Jake) and **Frank McKeown** are cofounders of *5 oceans, inc.* and codevelopers of Real Time Strategic Change. They support people worldwide in rapidly creating sustainable preferred futures. Their combined consulting experience represents over two decades of work with Fortune 500 companies, government, communities, and nonprofits.

Jake is the author of *Real Time Strategic Change: How to Involve an Entire Organization in Fast and Far-Reaching Change* (Berrett-Koehler, 1994). His belief in people's ability to create their collective future is a core conviction that shapes his life and practice.

Frank has a background in both the natural and social sciences, working for many years in both the private and public sectors prior to consulting. His abiding interest in sustainable land use, strategy, and values development influences his current work.

This chapter includes the consideration and thinking of many members of the RTSC Global Learning Community. The authors want to thank Marie Tyvoll, who partnered closely with them and brought ideas, energy, and clarity to this project.

Jake and Frank can be reached at (734) 475-4215 or info@5oceans.com.

Series Editors
Peggy Holman is a writer and consultant who helps organizations achieve cultural transformation. High involvement and a whole-systems perspective characterize her work. Her clients include AT&T Wireless

Services, Weyerhaeuser Company, St. Joseph's Medical Center, and the U.S. Department of Labor. Peggy can be reached at (425) 746-6274 or pholman@msn.com

Tom Devane is an internationally known consultant and speaker specializing in transformation. He helps companies plan and implement transformations that utilize highly participative methods to achieve sustainable change. His clients include Microsoft, Hewlett-Packard, AT&T, Johnson & Johnson, and the Republic of South Africa. Tom can be reached at (303) 898-6172 or tdevane@iex.net.

THE CHANGE HANDBOOK
Group Methods for Shaping the Future
◆

Edited by Peggy Holman and Tom Devane

The Change Handbook presents 18 proven change methods together in one volume so that readers can can learn about the diverse array of methods being successfully employed today and choose the method that will work best for them.

Each method is described in a separate chapter, written by its creator or an expert practitioner. Once readers determine which method is most compatible with their organizations, the book's comprehensive resource section provides books, articles, organizations, Internet sites, individuals, and other sources that can help get them up and running.

For managers starting out in a new change effort, this book provides a number of fresh-start alternatives. For organizations that want to revive stalled reengineering, Total Quality initiatives, or large information technology projects, this book provides a complete menu of workable options.

CONTENTS

Peggy Holman works with organizations to transform their culture using a variety of approaches involving organizational learning and Total Quality Management. She has worked with a wide range of companies including US WEST Cellular, US WEST Communications, Weyerhaeuser Company, St. Joseph's Medical Center, and AT&T Wireless Services.

Tom Devane helps organizations plan and implement transformations that utilize highly participative methods to achieve sustainable change. His clients have included Microsoft, Hewlett-Packard, AT&T, Johnson & Johnson, US West, and the Republic of South Africa.

Paperback original, Approx. 500 pages, 7x10, ISBN 1-57675-058-2
Item no. 50582-605 US $39.95 (CAN $57.95)
To order call 800-929-2929 or visit www.bkconnection.com

Collaborating for Change

Peggy Holman and Tom Devane, Editors

The Collaborating for Change booklet series offers concise, comprehensive overviews of 14 leading change strategies in a convenient, inexpensive format. Adapted from chapters in *The Change Handbook,* each booklet is written by the originator of the change strategy or an expert practitioner, and includes

- ◆ An example of the strategy in action
- ◆ Tips for getting started
- ◆ An outline of roles, responsibilities, and relationships
- ◆ Conditions for success
- ◆ Keys to sustaining results
- ◆ Thought-provoking questions for discussion

If you're deciding on a change strategy for your organization and you need a short, focused treatment of several alternatives to distribute to your colleagues, or you've decided on a change strategy and want to disseminate information about it to get everyone on board, the Collaborating for Change booklets are the ideal choice.

◆ SEARCH CONFERENCE
Merrelyn Emery and Tom Devane
Uses open systems principles in strategic planning, thereby creating a well-articulated, achievable future with identifiable goals, a timetable, and action plans for realizing that future.

◆ FUTURE SEARCH
Marvin R. Weisbord and Sandra Janoff
Helps members of an organization or community discover common ground and create self-managed plans to move toward their desired future.

◆ THE CONFERENCE MODEL
Emily M. Axelrod and Richard H. Axelrod
Engages the critical mass needed for success in redesigning organizations and processes, co-creating a vision of the future, improving customer and supplier relationships, or achieving strategic alignment.

◆ THE WHOLE SYSTEMS APPROACH
Cindy Adams and W. A. (Bill) Adams
Creates a world of work where people and organizations thrive and produce outrageous individual and organizational results.

◆ THE STRATEGIC FORUM
Chris Sonderquist
Answers "Can our strategy achieve our objectives?" by building shared understanding (a mental map) of how the organization or community really works.

◆ PARTICIPATIVE DESIGN WORKSHOP
Merrelyn Emery and Tom Devane
Enables an organization to function in an interrelated structure of self-managing work groups.

◆ GEMBA KAIZEN
Masaaki Imai and Brian Heymans
Builds a culture able to initiate and sustain change by providing skills to improve process, enabling employees to make daily improvements, installing JIT systems and lean process methods in administrative systems, and improving equipment reliability and product quality.

◆ THE ORGANIZATION WORKSHOP
Barry Oshry and Tom Devane
Develops the knowledge and skills of "system sight" that enable us to create partnerships up, down, and across organizational lines.

◆ WHOLE-SCALE CHANGE
Kathleen D. Dannemiller, Sylvia L. James, and Paul D. Tolchinsky
Helps organizations remain successful through fast, deep, and sustainable total system change by bringing members together as one-brain (all seeing the same things) and one-heart (all committed to achieving the same preferred future).

◆ OPEN SPACE TECHNOLOGY
Harrison Owen (with Anne Stadler)
Enables high levels of group interaction and productivity to provide a basis for enhanced organizational function over time.

◆ APPRECIATIVE INQUIRY
David L. Cooperrider and Diana Whitney
Supports full-voiced appreciative participation in order to tap an organization's positive change core and inspire collaborative action that serves the whole system.

◆ THINK LIKE A GENIUS PROCESS
Todd Siler
Helps individuals and organizations go beyond narrow, compartmentalized thinking; improve communication, teamwork, and collaboration; and achieve breakthrough thinking.

◆ REAL TIME STRATEGIC CHANGE
Ronald W. Jacobs and Frank McKeown
Uses large, interactive group meetings to rapidly create an organization's preferred future and then sustain it over time.

Collaborating for Change Order Form
Each booklet comes shrinkwrapped in packets of 6

Order in Quantity and Save!
1–4 packets: $45 per packet • 5–9 packets: $40.50 per packet
10–49 packets: $38.25 per packet • 50–99 packets: $36 per packet

# of Packets		Item #	Price
_____	Search Conference	6058X-605	_____
_____	Future Search	60598-605	_____
_____	The Strategic Forum	60601-605	_____
_____	Participative Design Workshop	6061X-605	_____
_____	Gemba Kaizen	60628-605	_____
_____	The Whole Systems Approach	60636-605	_____
_____	Preferred Futuring	60644-605	_____
_____	The Organization Workshop	60652-605	_____
_____	Whole-Scale Change	60660-605	_____
_____	Open Space Technology	60679-605	_____
_____	Appreciative Inquiry	60687-605	_____
_____	The Conference Model	60695-605	_____
_____	Think Like a Genius Process	60709-605	_____
_____	Real Time Strategic Change	60717-605	_____

Shipping and Handling _____
($4.50 for the first packet; $1.50 for each additional packet.)

TOTAL (CA residents add sales tax) $_____

Method of Payment
Orders payable in U.S. dollars. Orders outside U.S. and Canada must be prepaid.

❏ Payment enclosed ❏ Visa ❏ MasterCard ❏ American Express

Card no. _____ Expiration date _____

Signature _____

Name _____ Title _____

Organization _____

Address _____

City/State/Zip _____

Phone (in case we have questions about your order) _____

May we notify you about new Berrett-Koehler products and special offers via e-mail?

E-mail _____

Send Orders to Berrett-Koehler Communications, Inc., P.O. Box 565,
Williston VT 05495 • **Fax** (802) 864-7626 • **Phone** (800) 929-2929
• **Web** www.bkconnection.com